AF265851

To Hannah Brielle, Our daughter whom we never held in our arms but held deep in our hearts and briefly in my body.

I felt you and knew you and cannot wait to see you again in Glory!
To Our sons and daughters in law/love,
You are definitely our rainbows in life and love!

You are the twinkle in your dad's eye still and held deeply in my heart!

Donesa Walker, M. Ed.
LearningRx of Shreveport
Master Reading/Dyslexia Specialist
Board Certified Cognitive Specialist
#BCCS206959

Heart Twinkle

So nice to finally
meet you sweet baby
of this birth

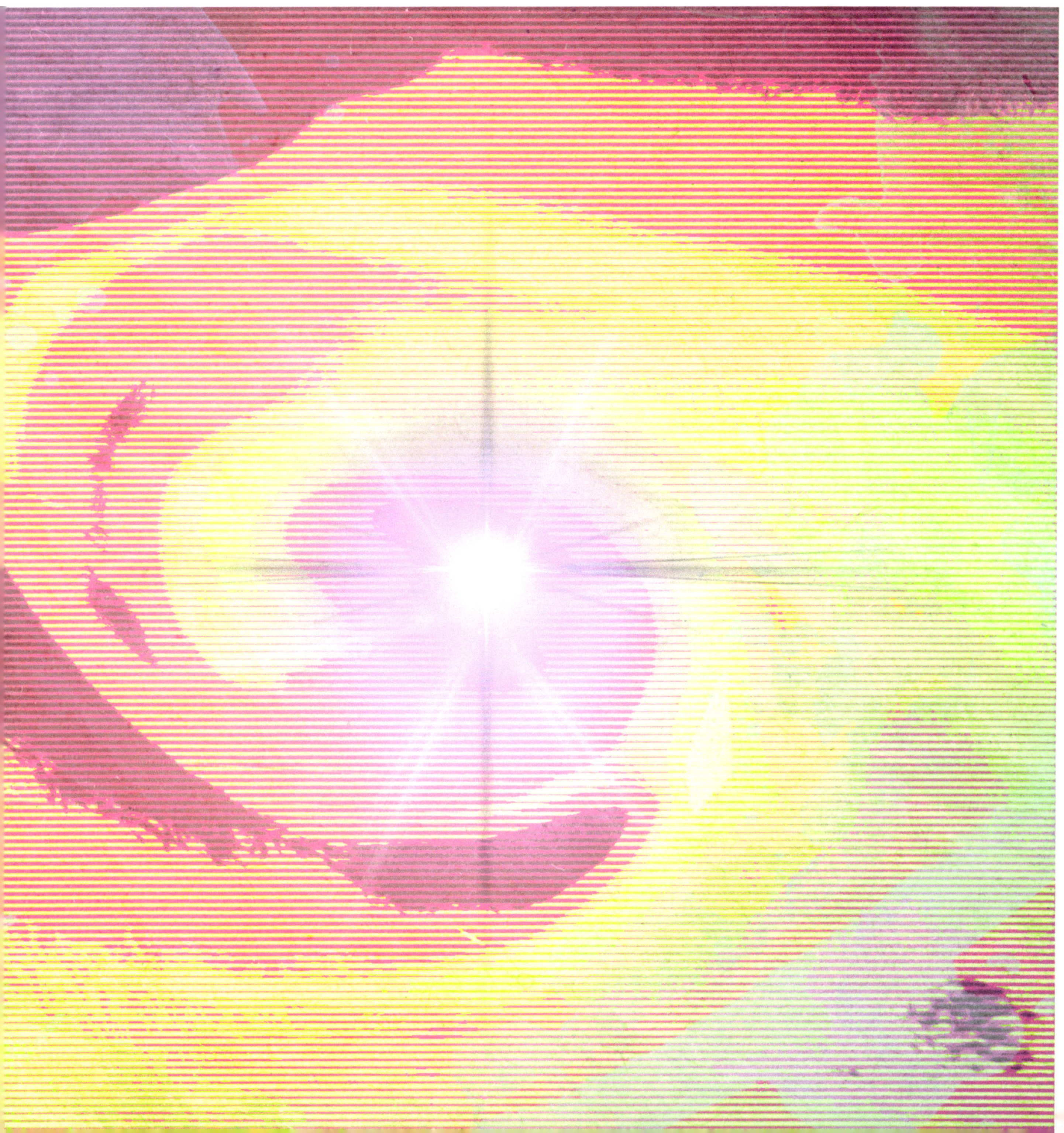

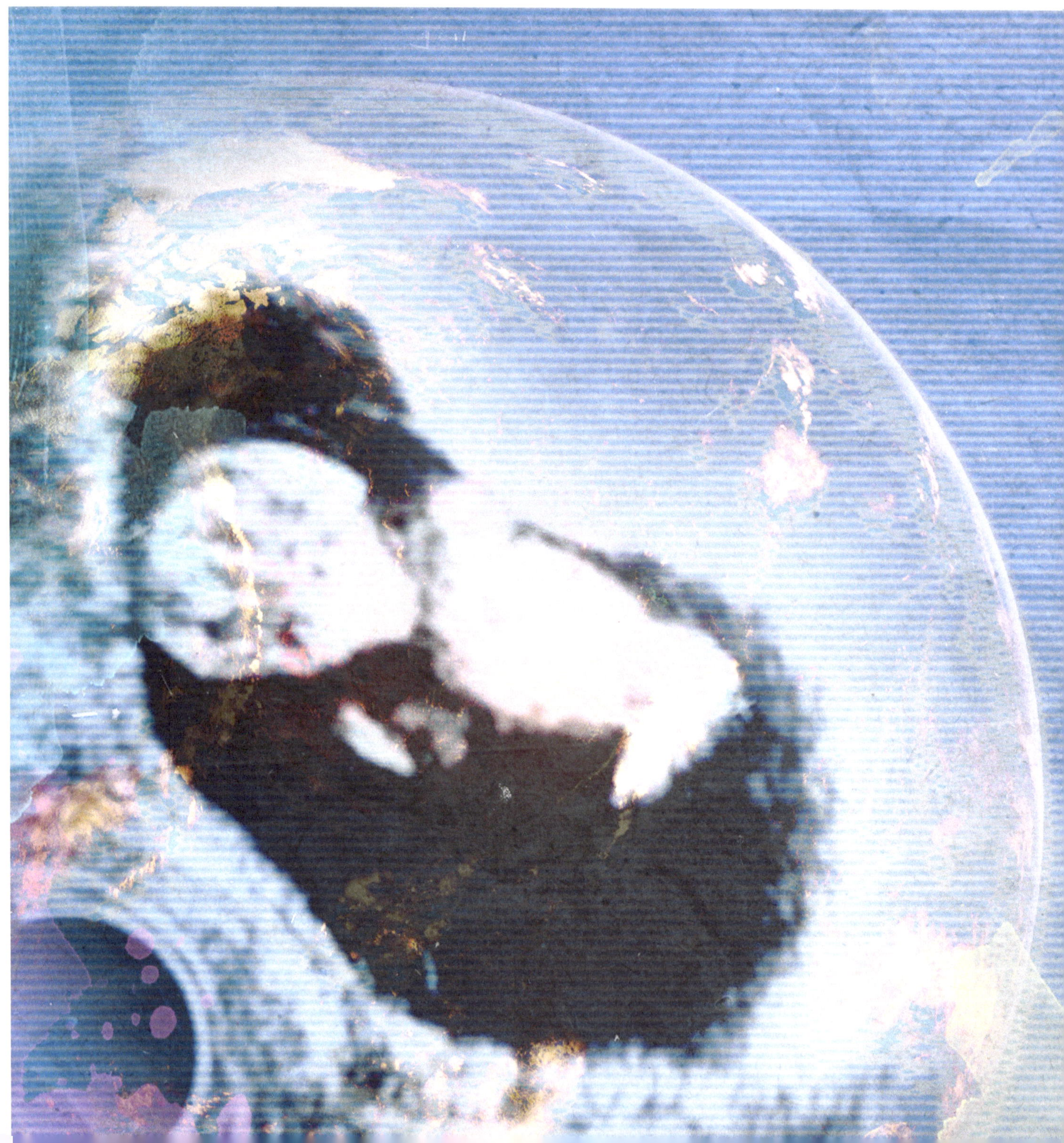

I am the one who
went before you
Though I quickly
left this Earth

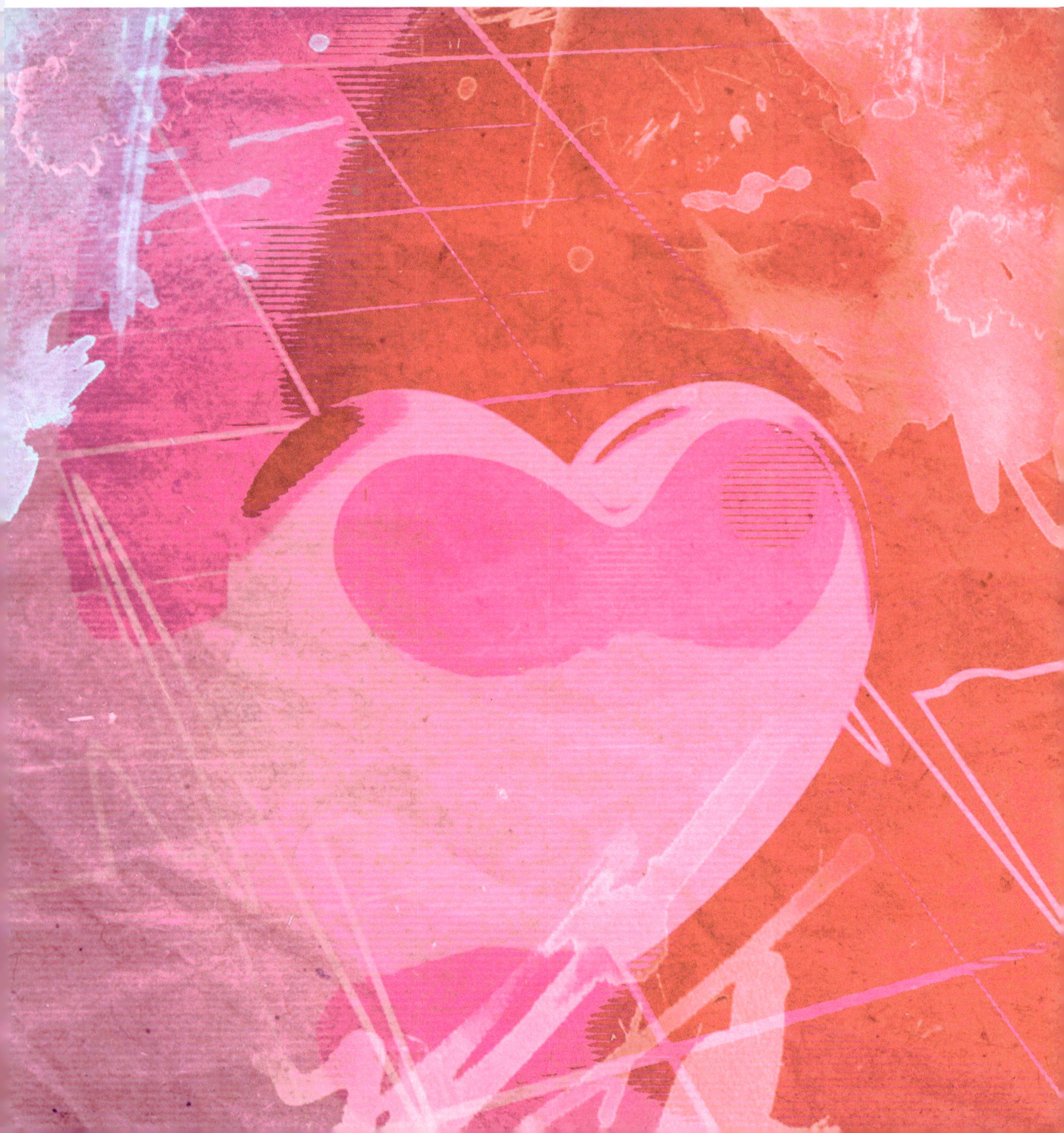

My heartbeat was
the first one
Momma heard inside

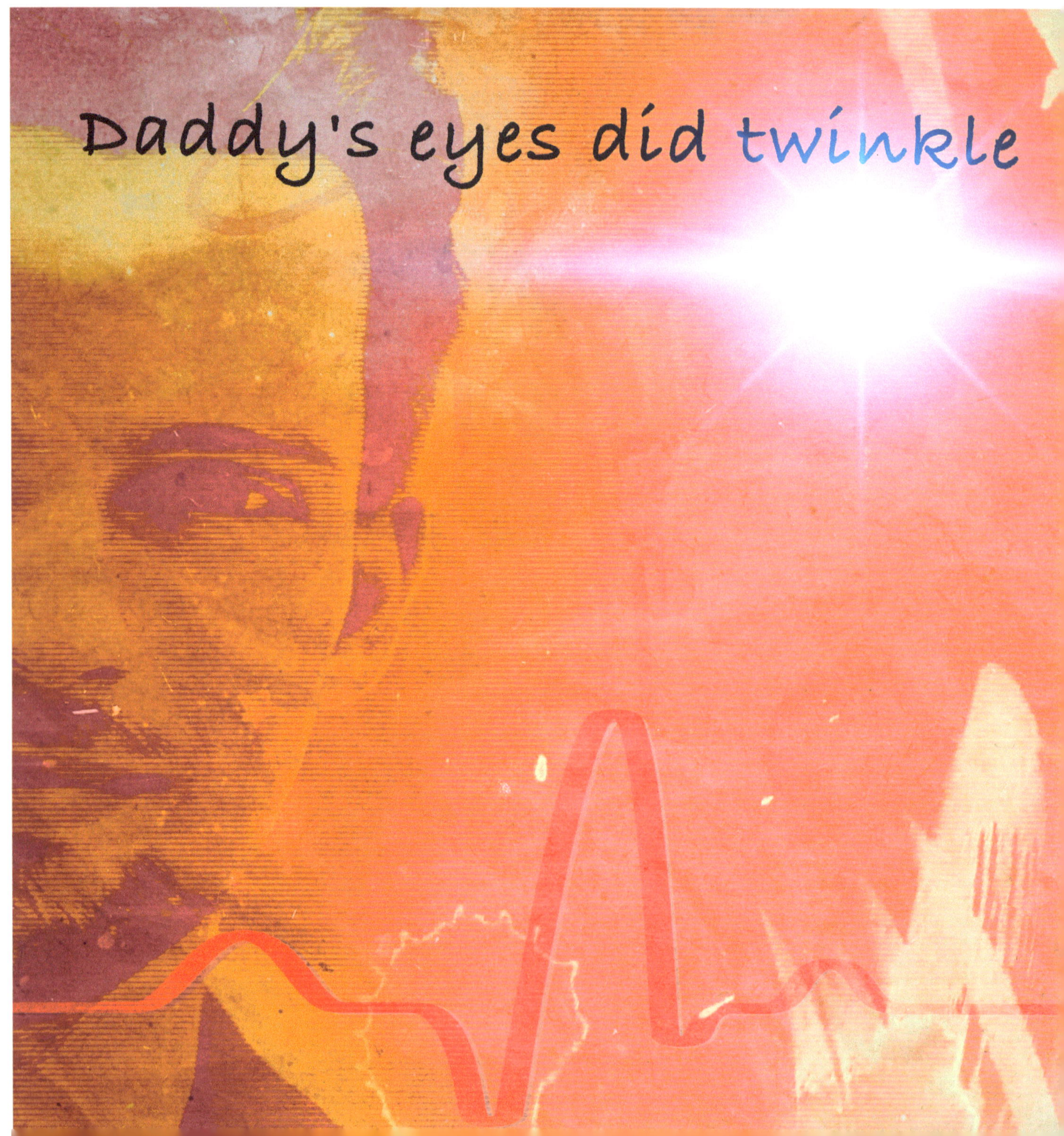
Daddy's eyes did twinkle

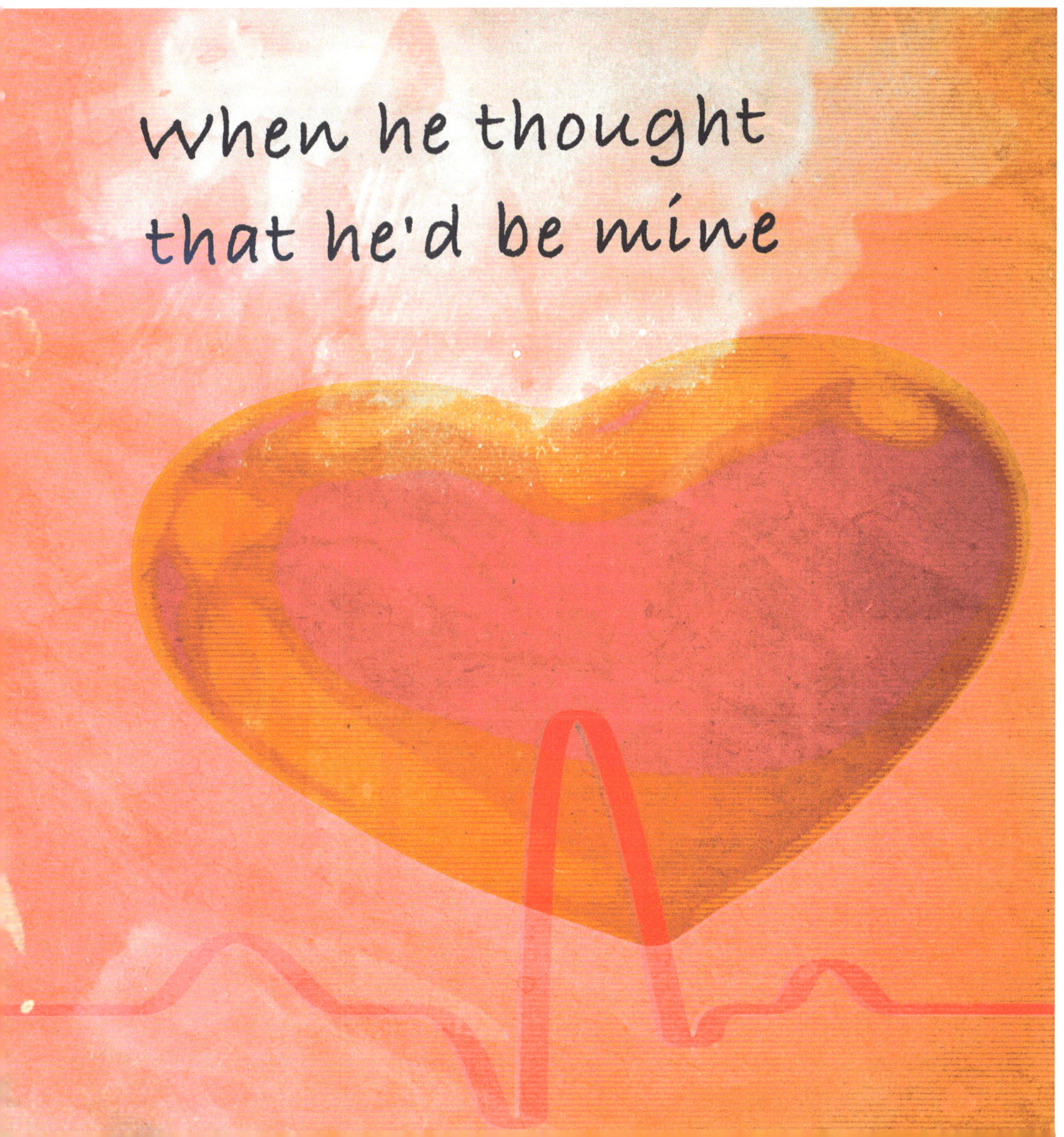
when he thought
that he'd be mine

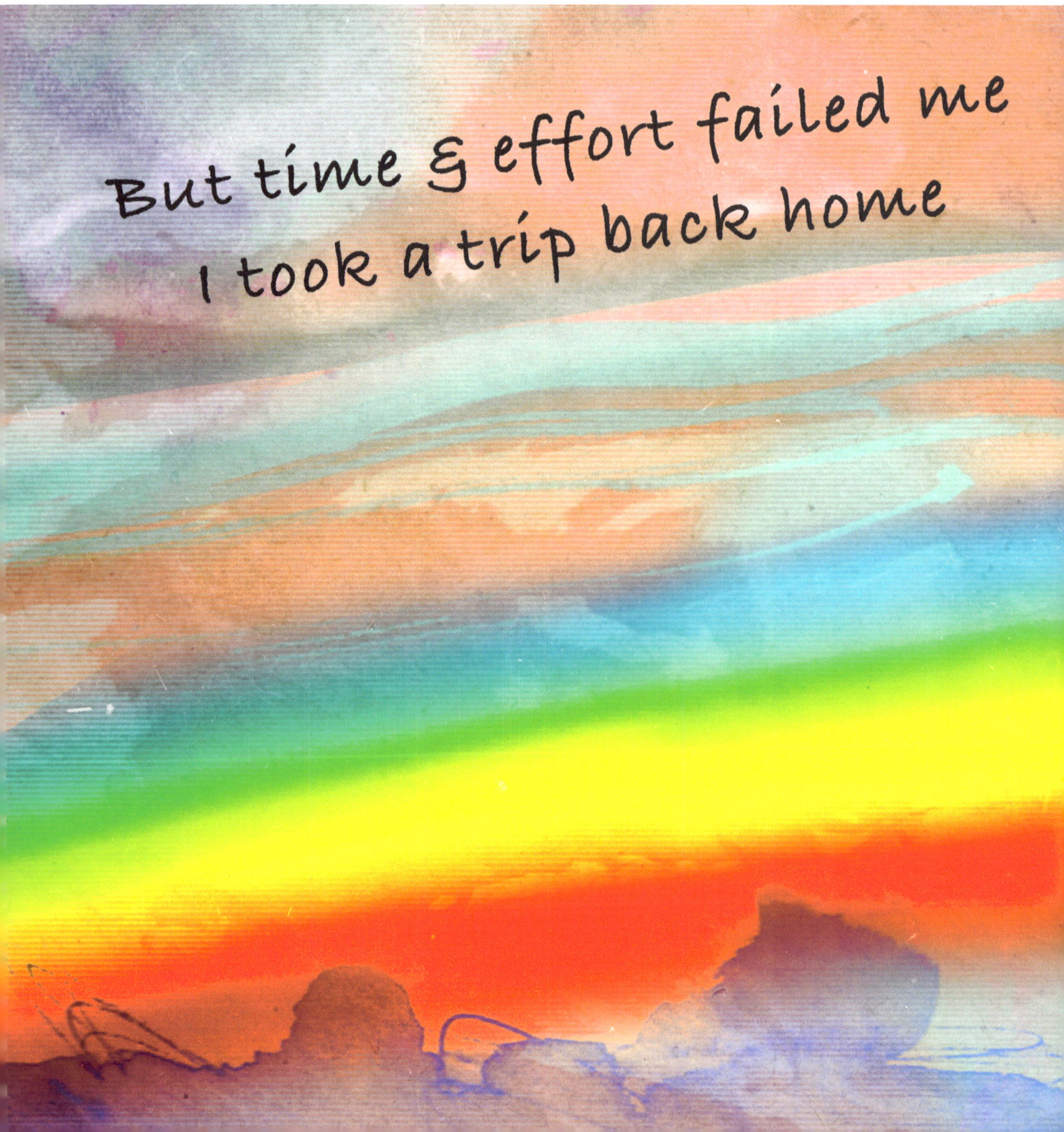
But time & effort failed me
I took a trip back home

God chose to keep me close to Him
In a place I wouldn't roam

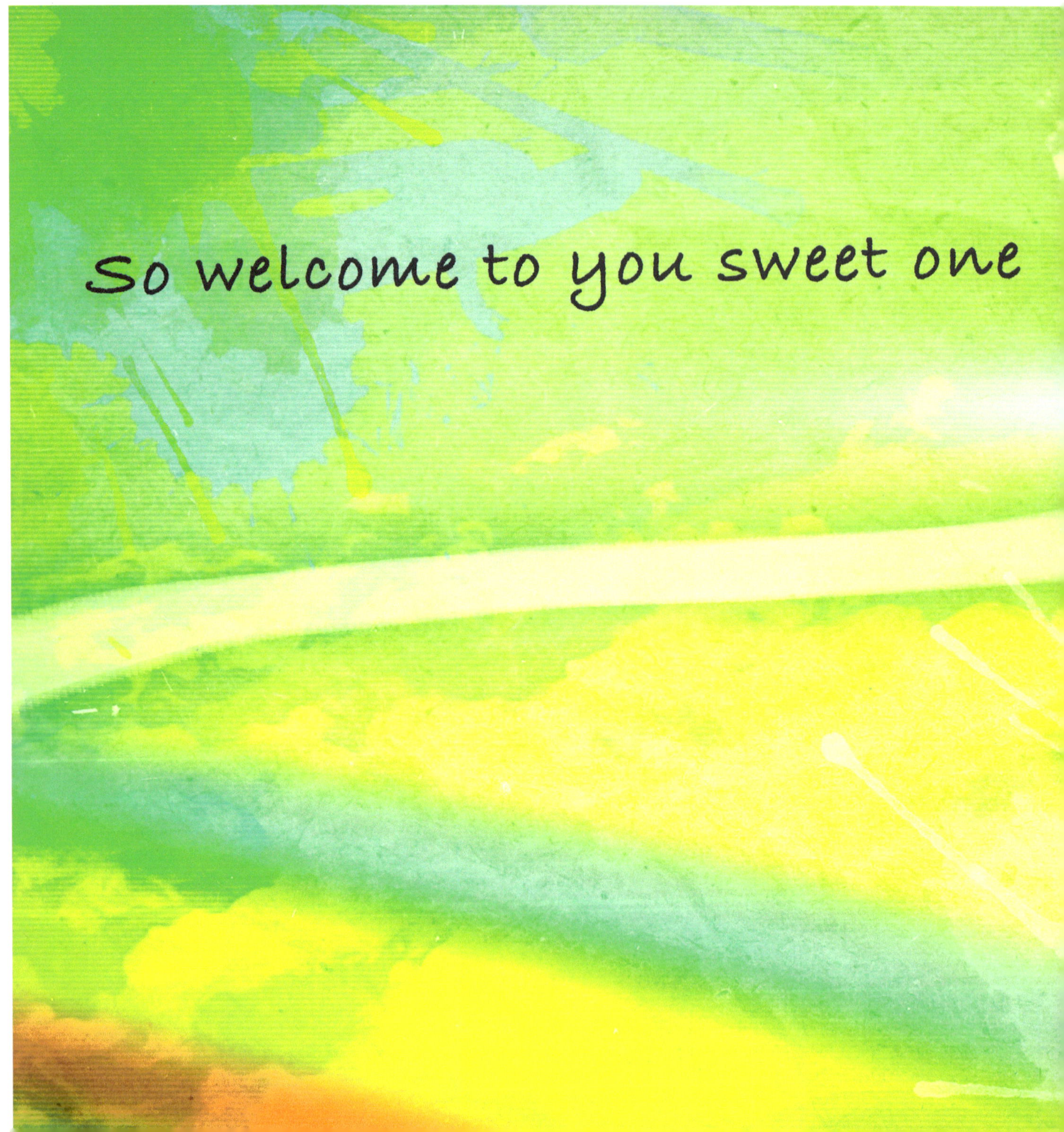

so welcome to you sweet one

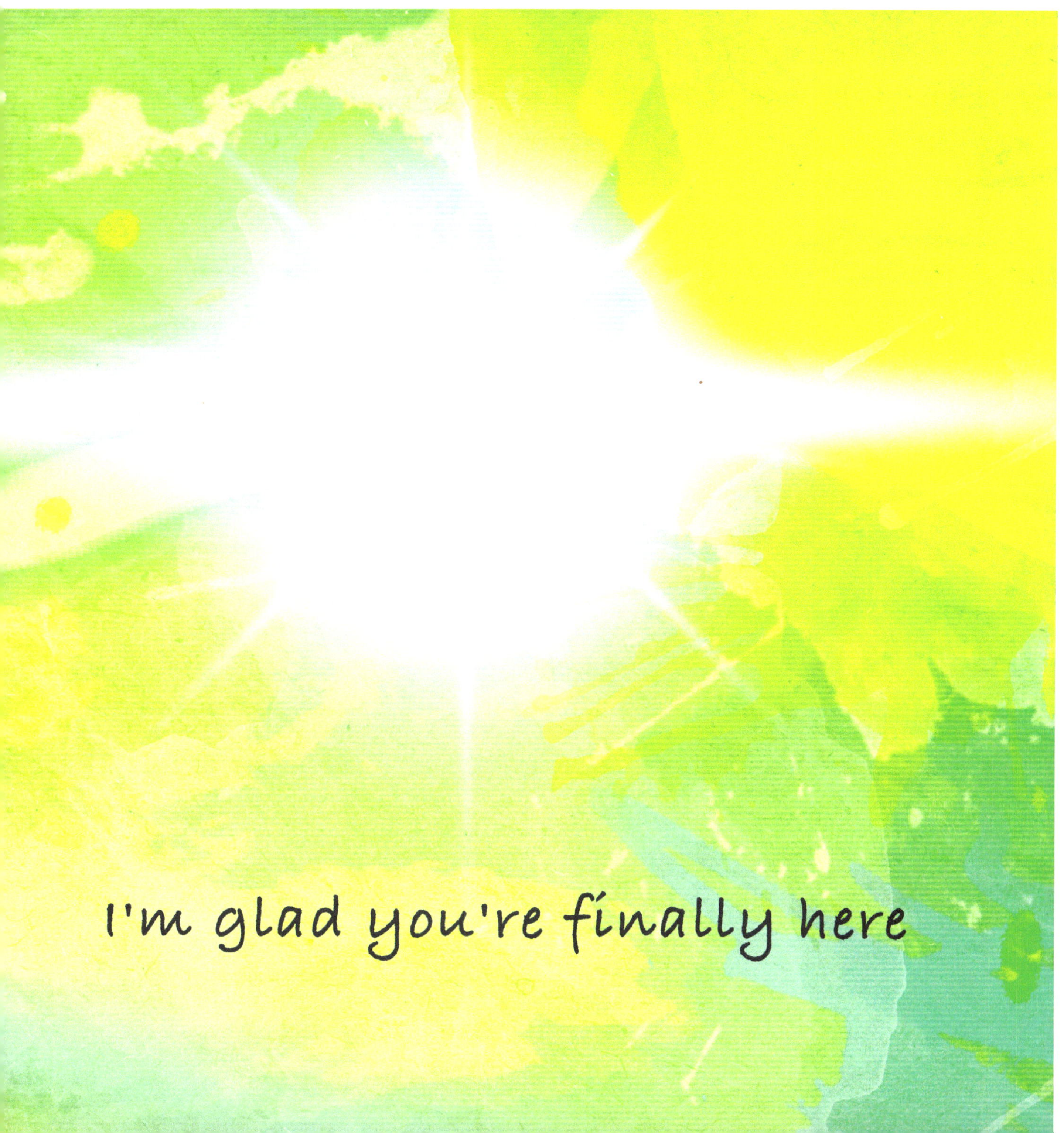

I'm glad you're finally here

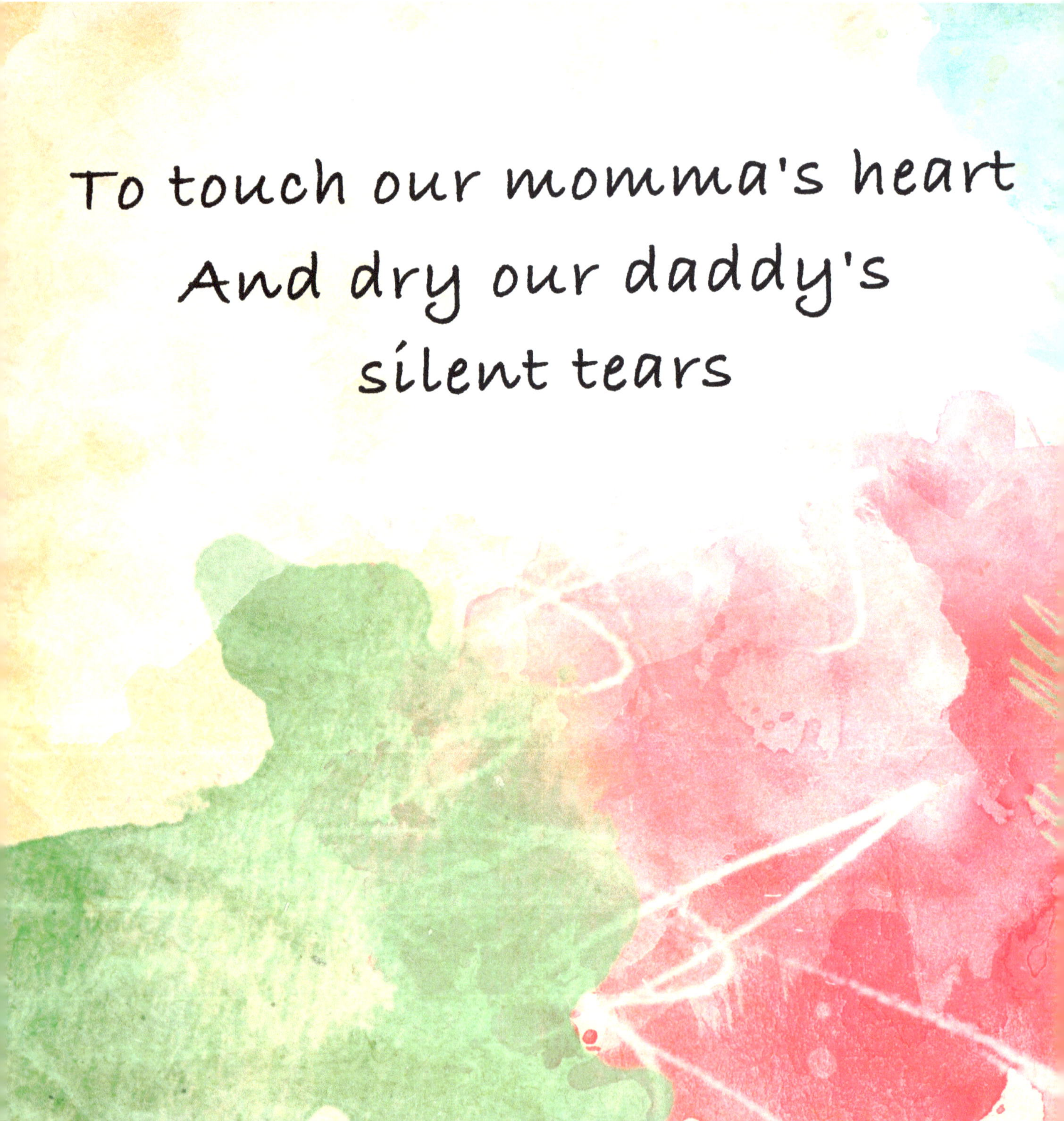
To touch our momma's heart
And dry our daddy's
silent tears

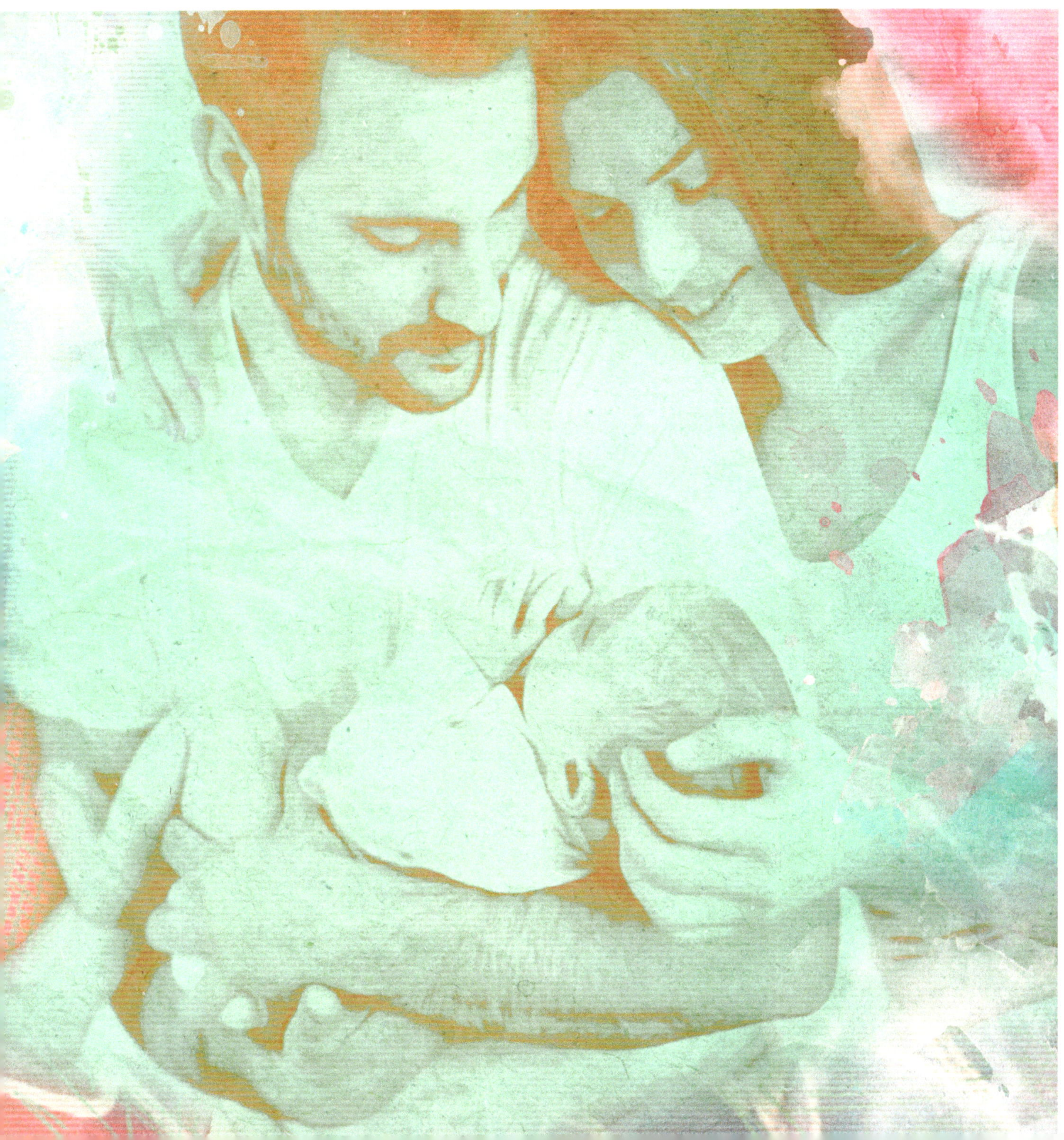

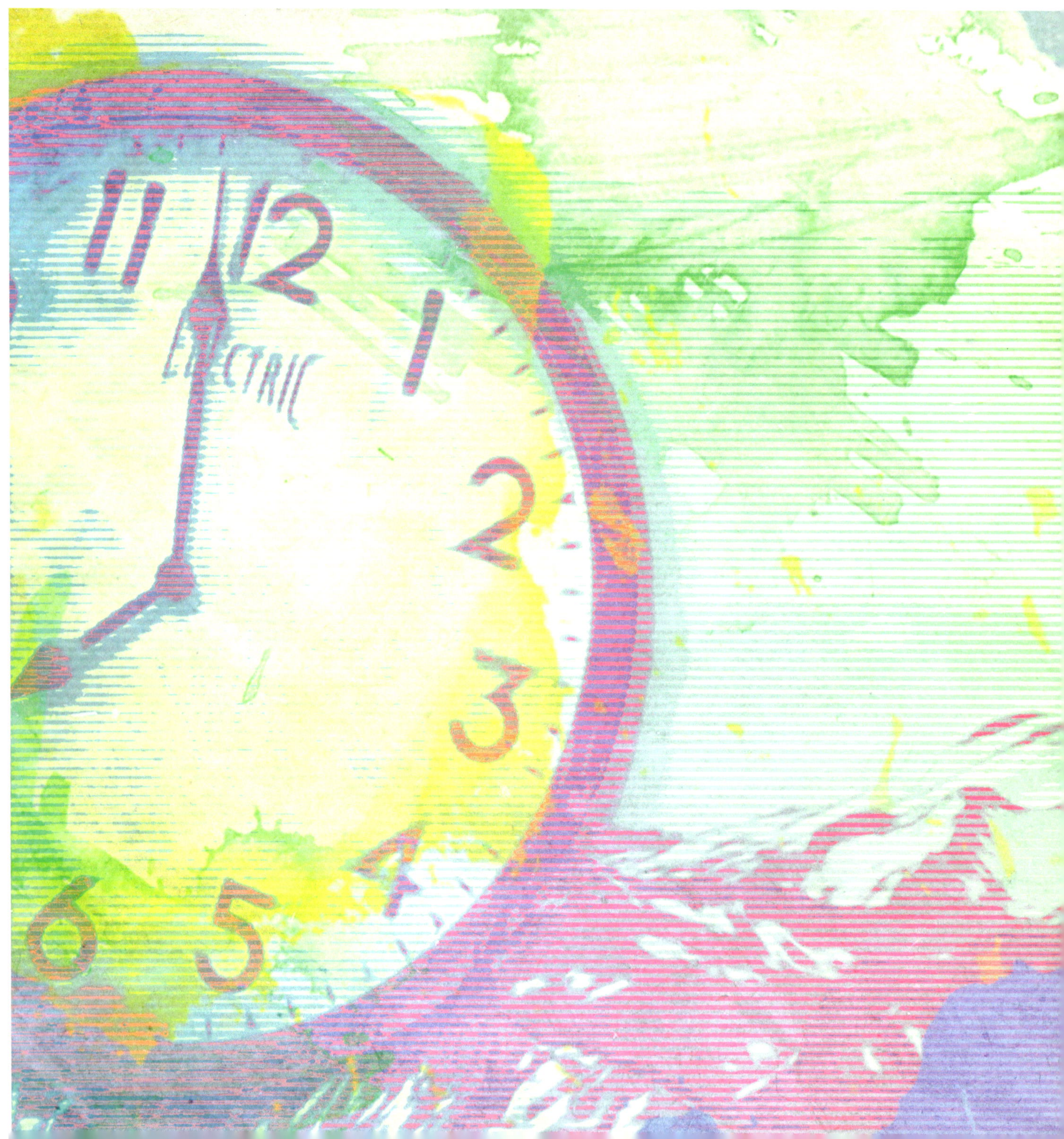

11
12
1
2
3
5
6
ELECTRIC

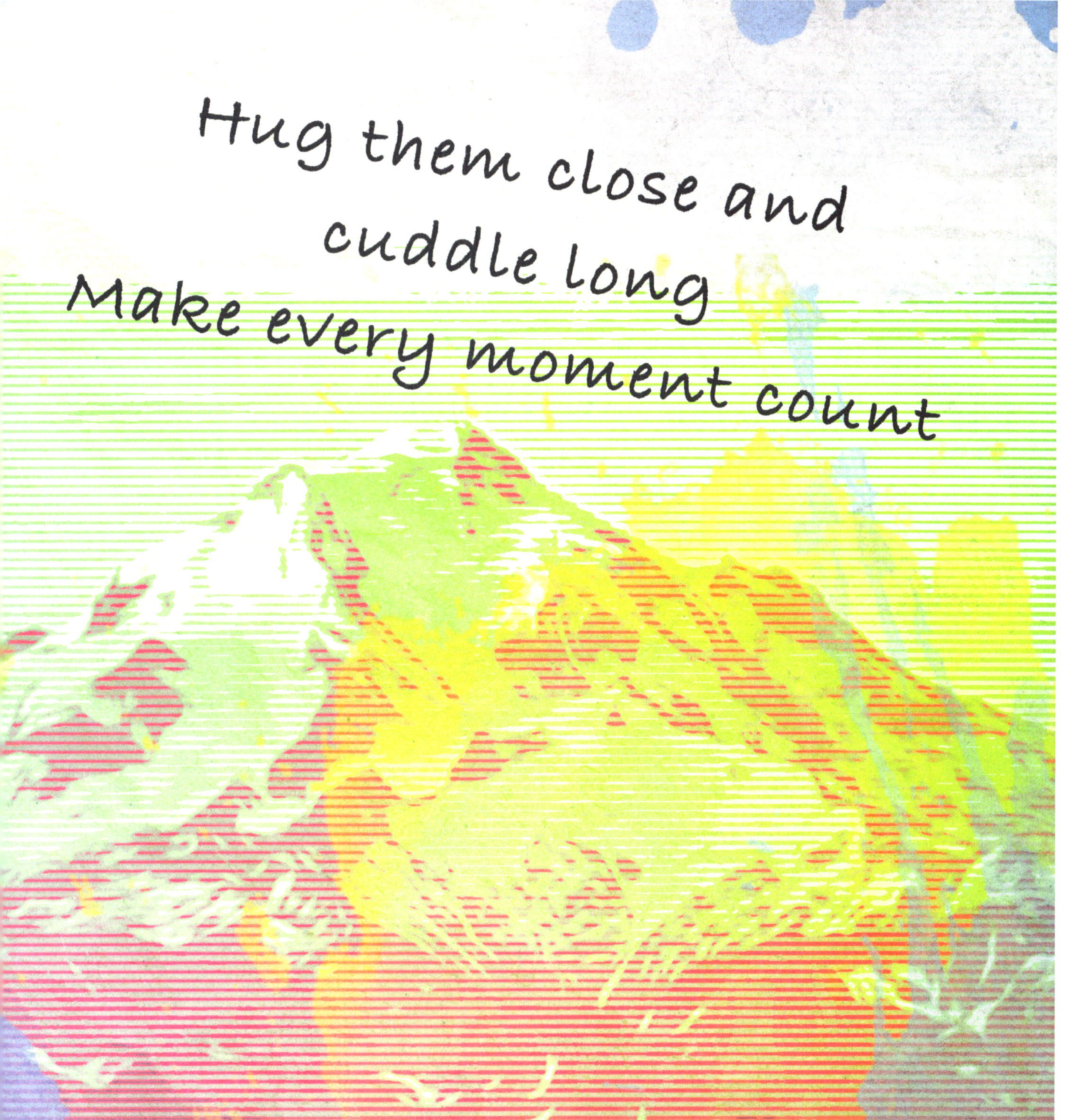

Hug them close and
cuddle long
Make every moment count

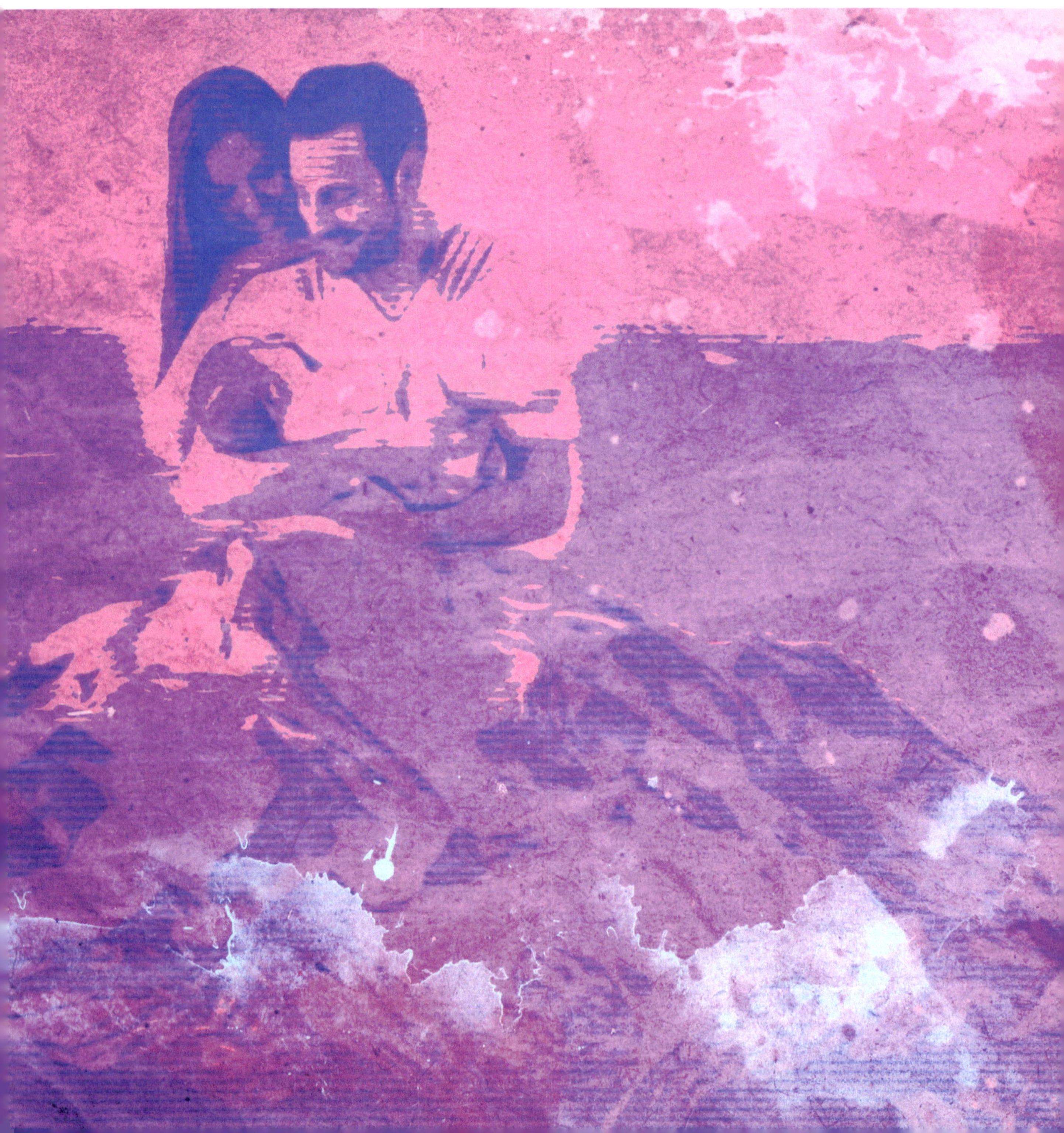

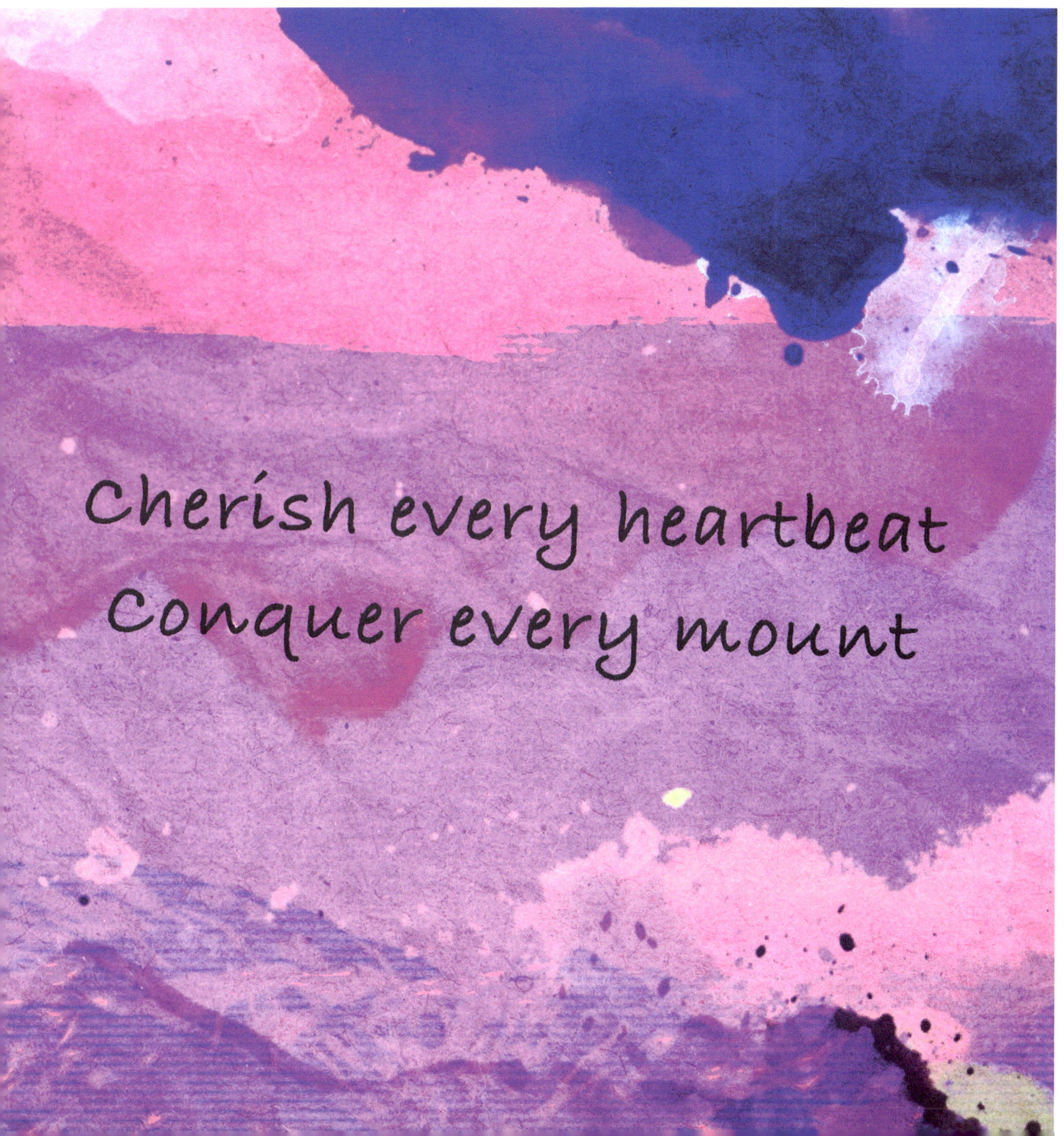

Cherish every heartbeat
Conquer every mount

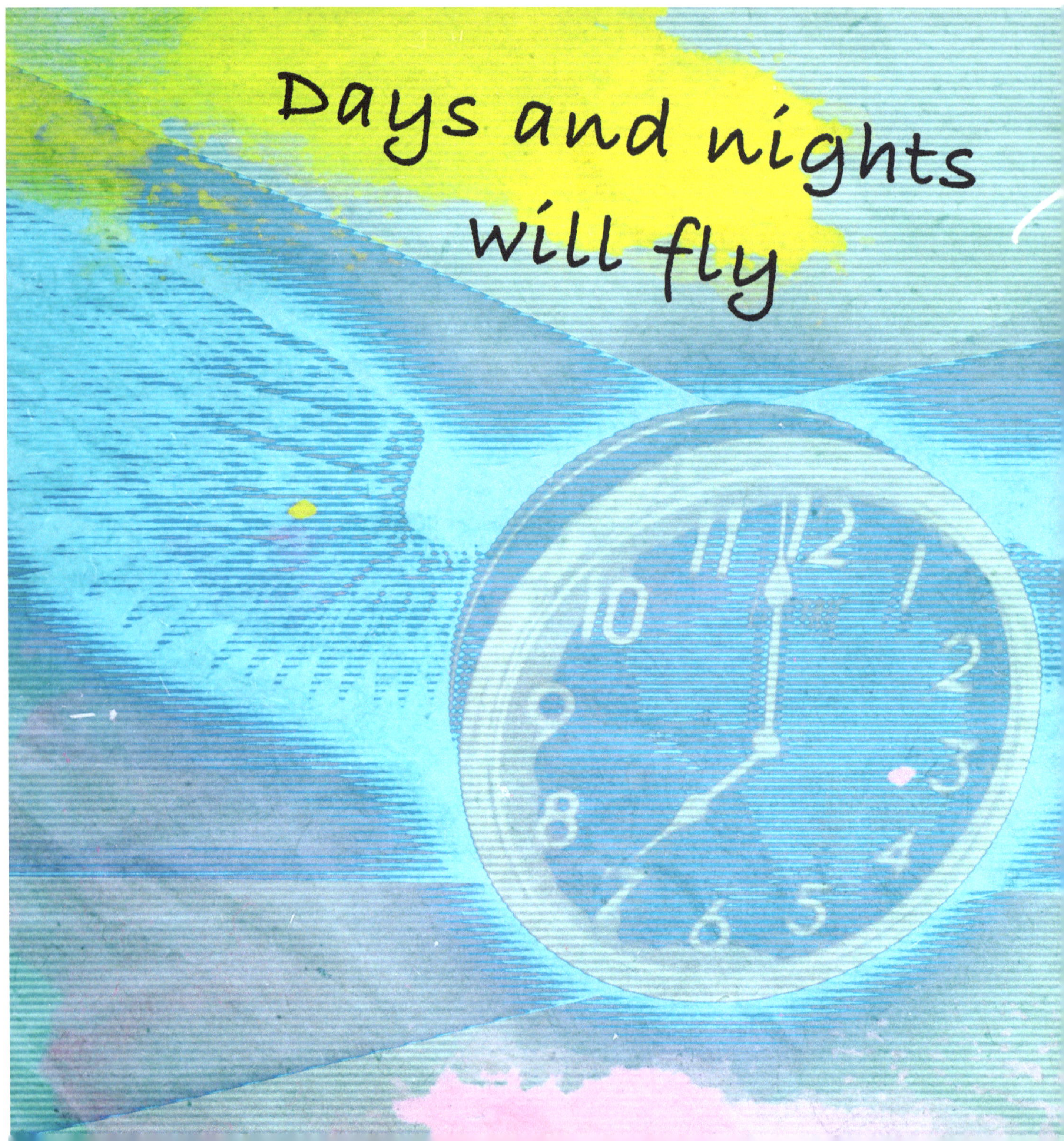
Days and nights
will fly

right past
the moments
of your life

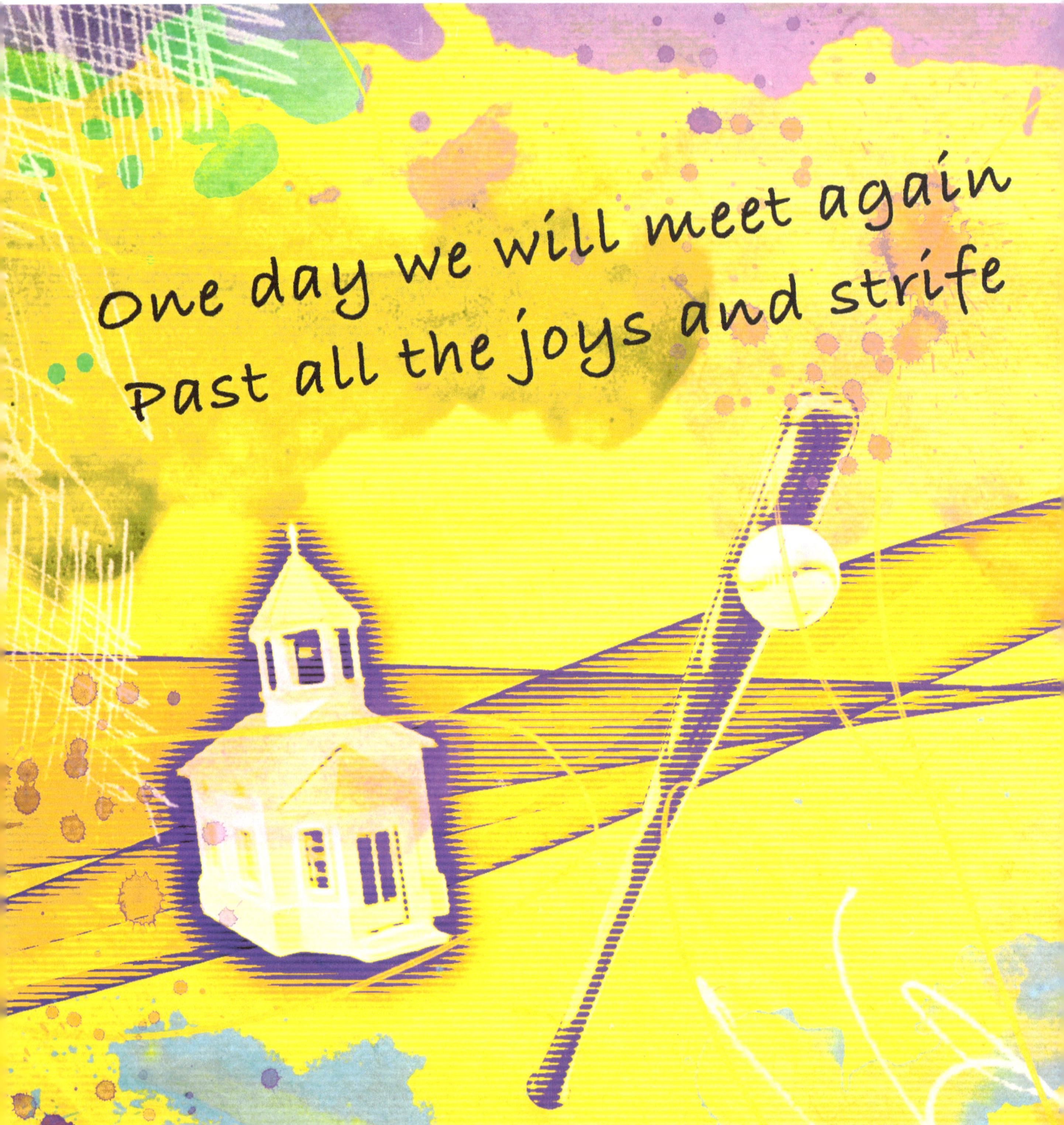

One day we will meet again
Past all the joys and strife

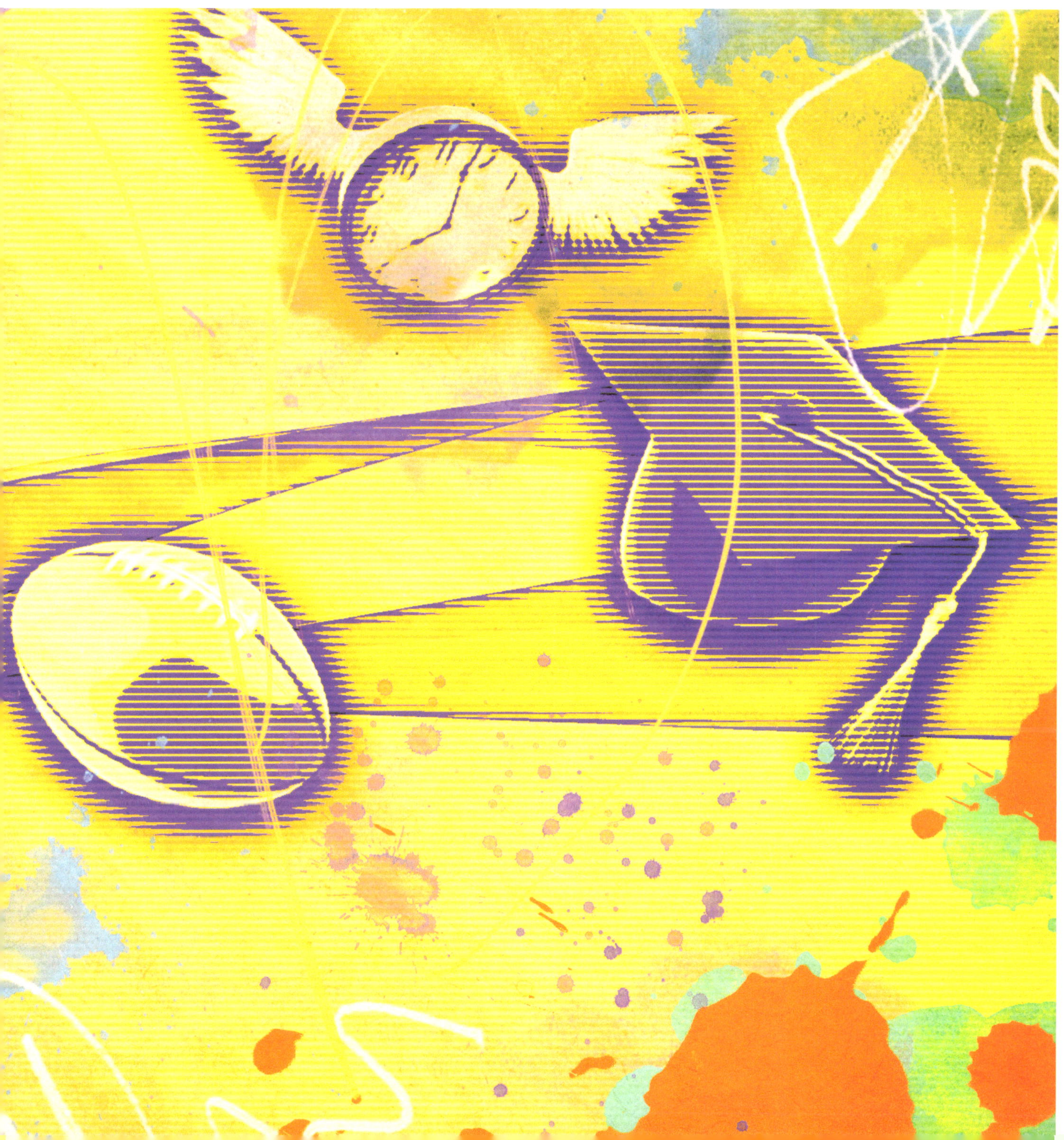

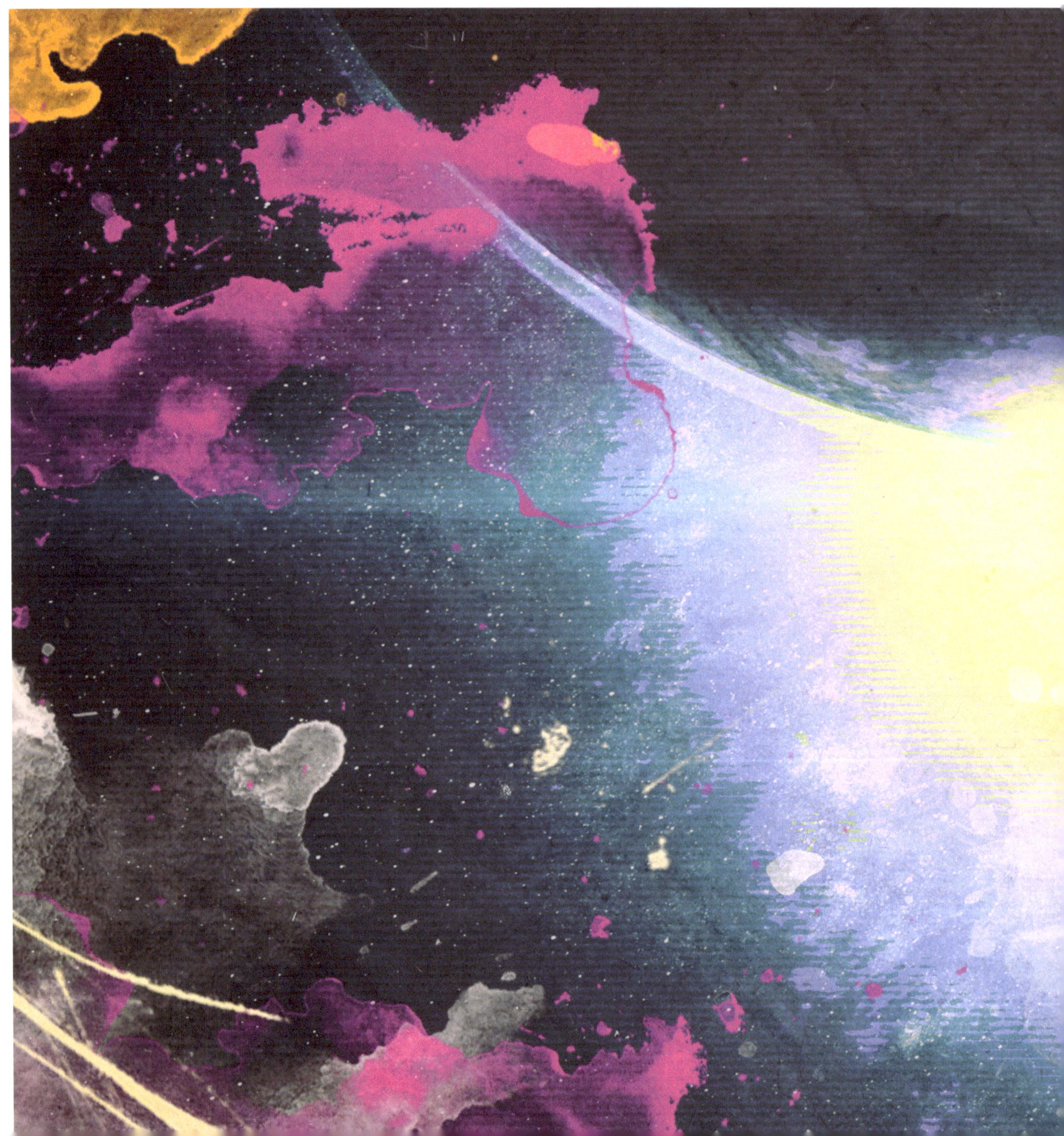

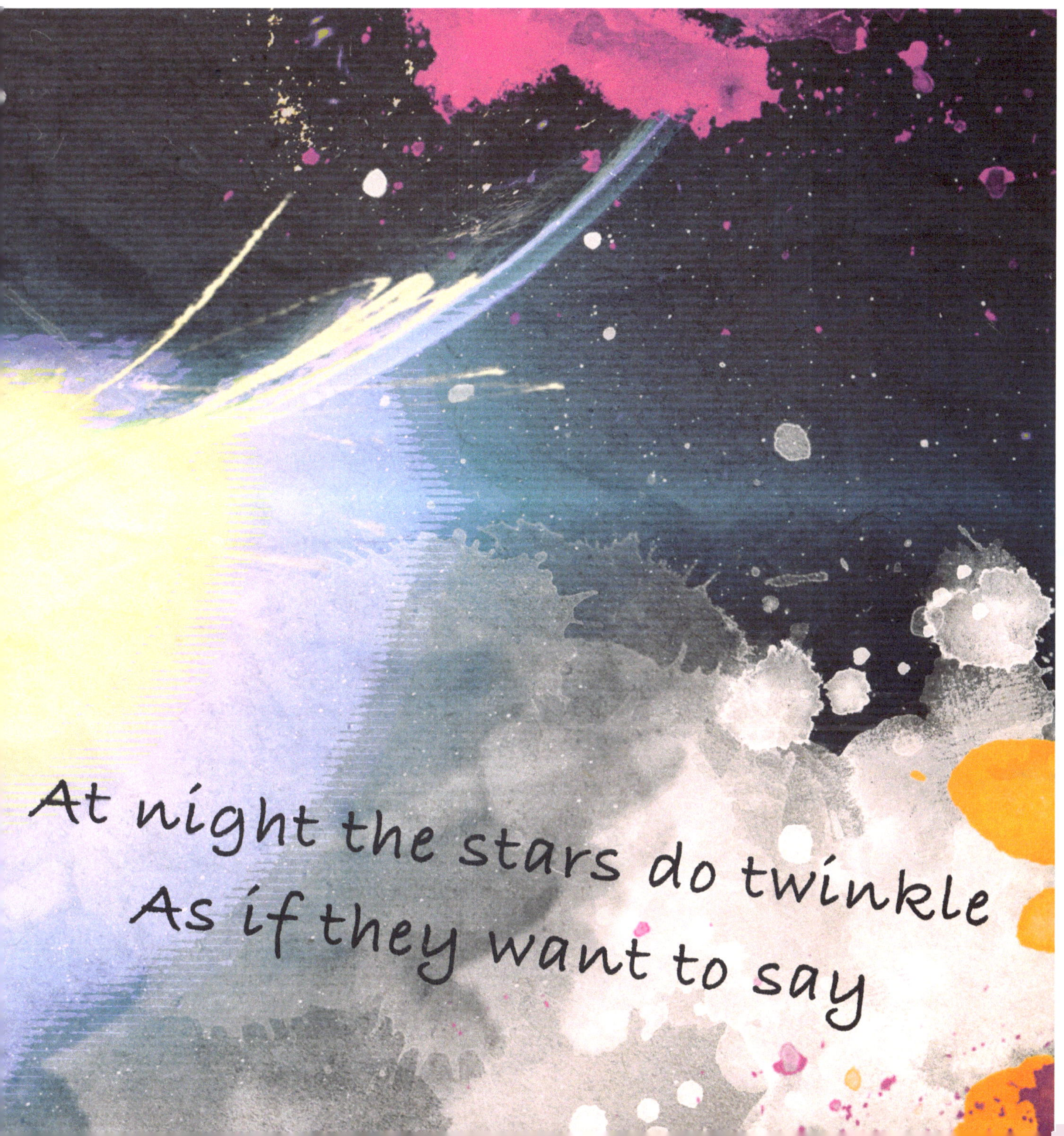
At night the stars do twinkle
As if they want to say

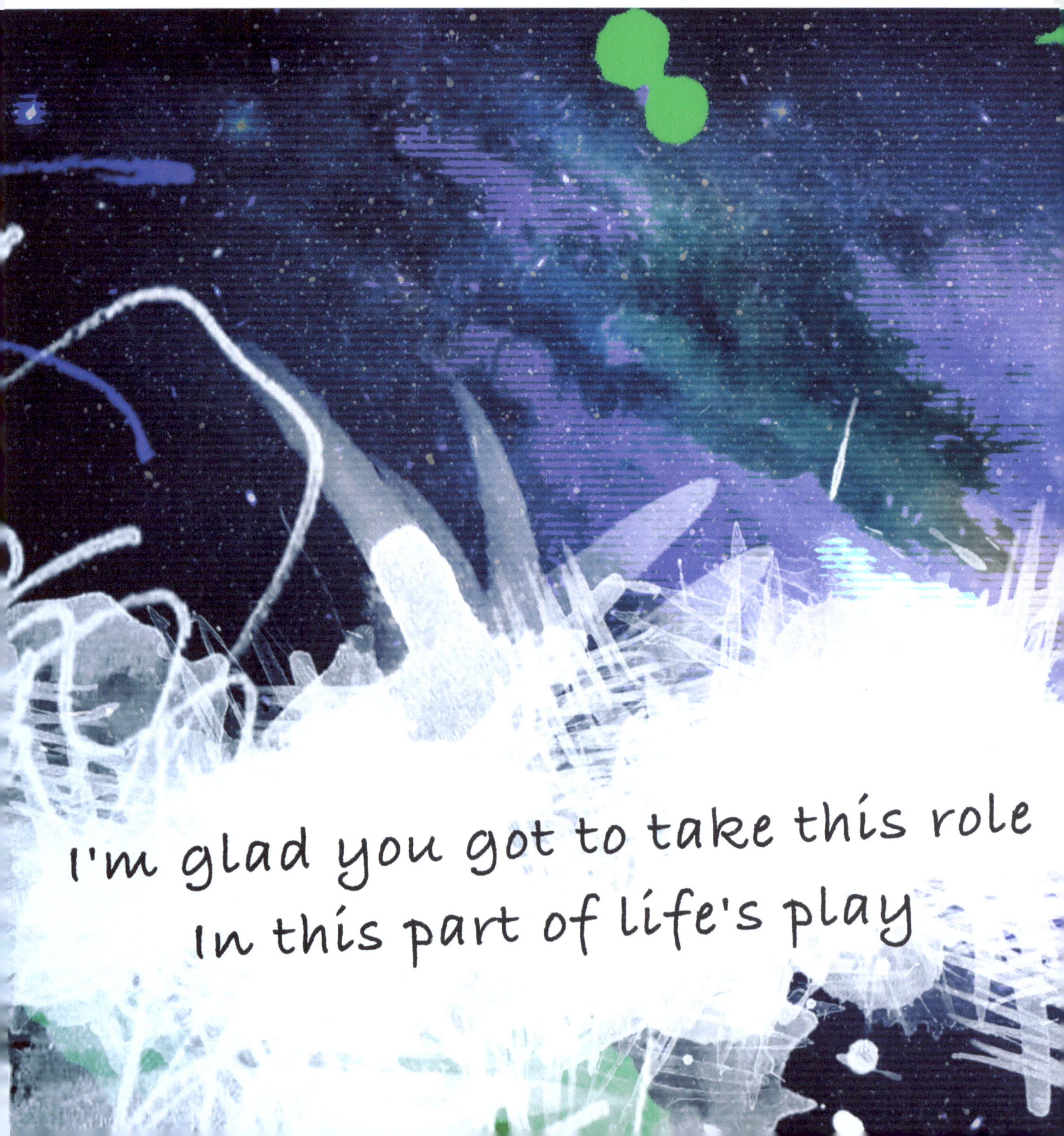

I'm glad you got to take this role
in this part of life's play

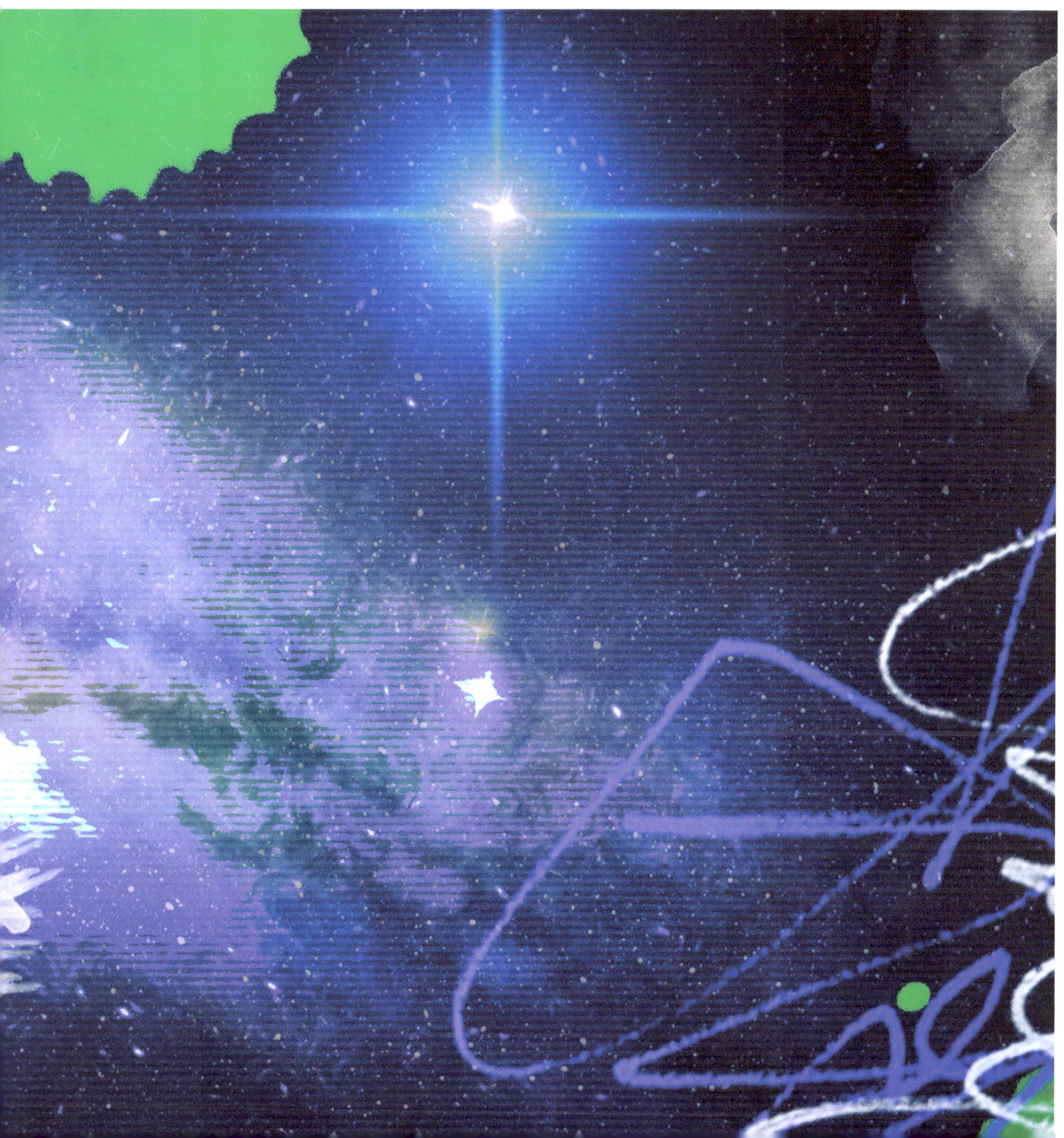

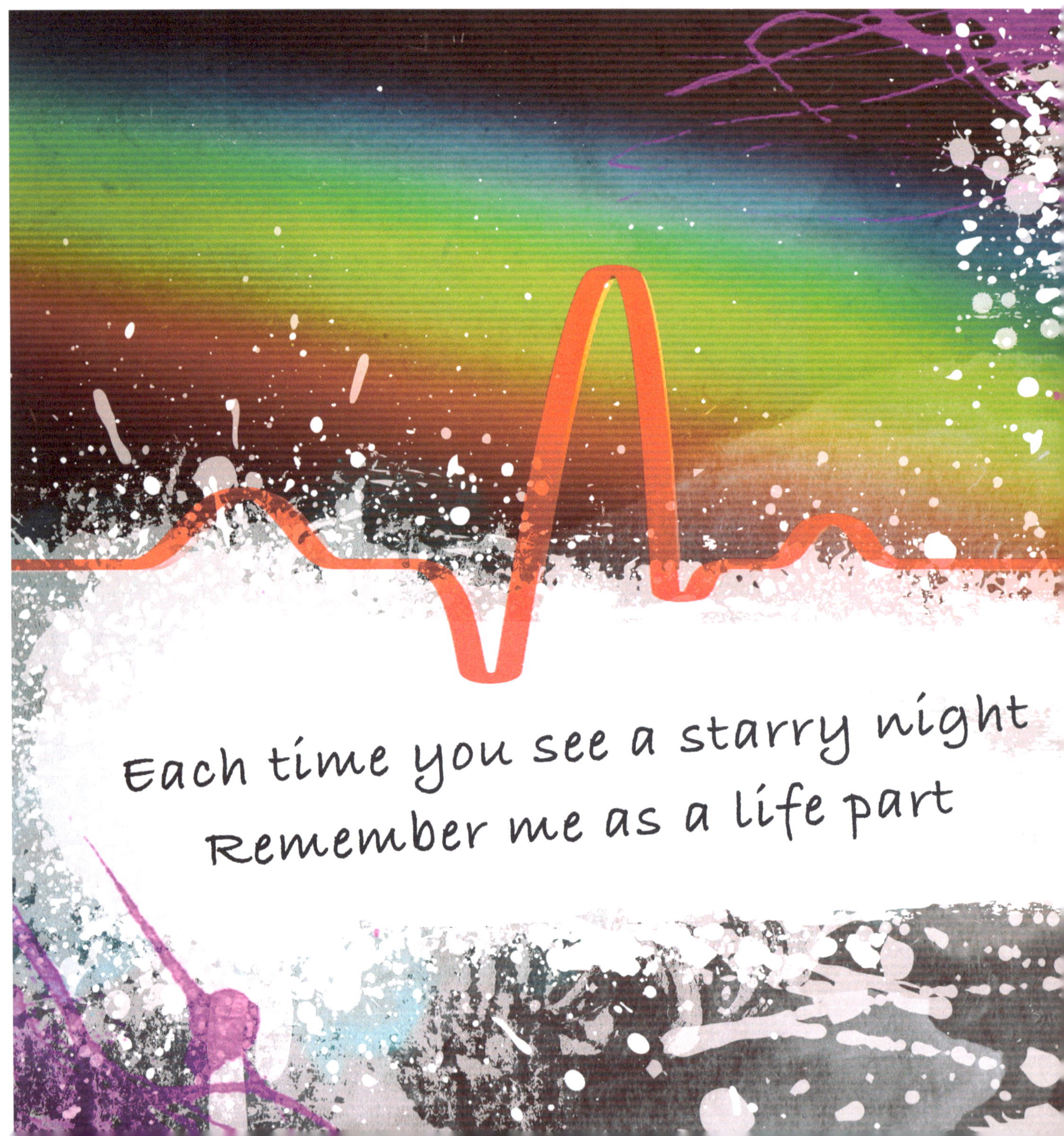
Each time you see a starry night
Remember me as a life part

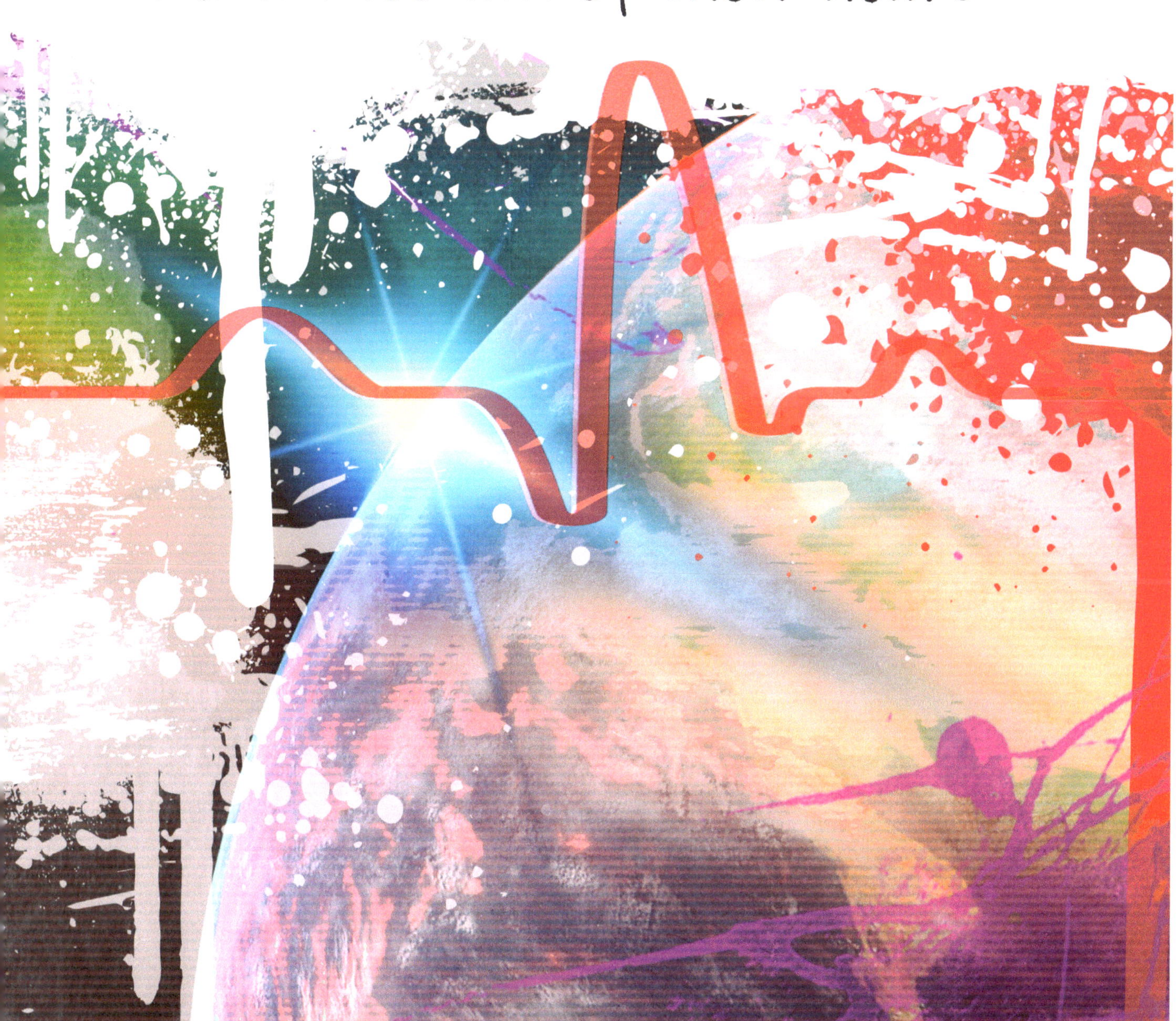
For mommy and daddy adore you
And I too am of their heart

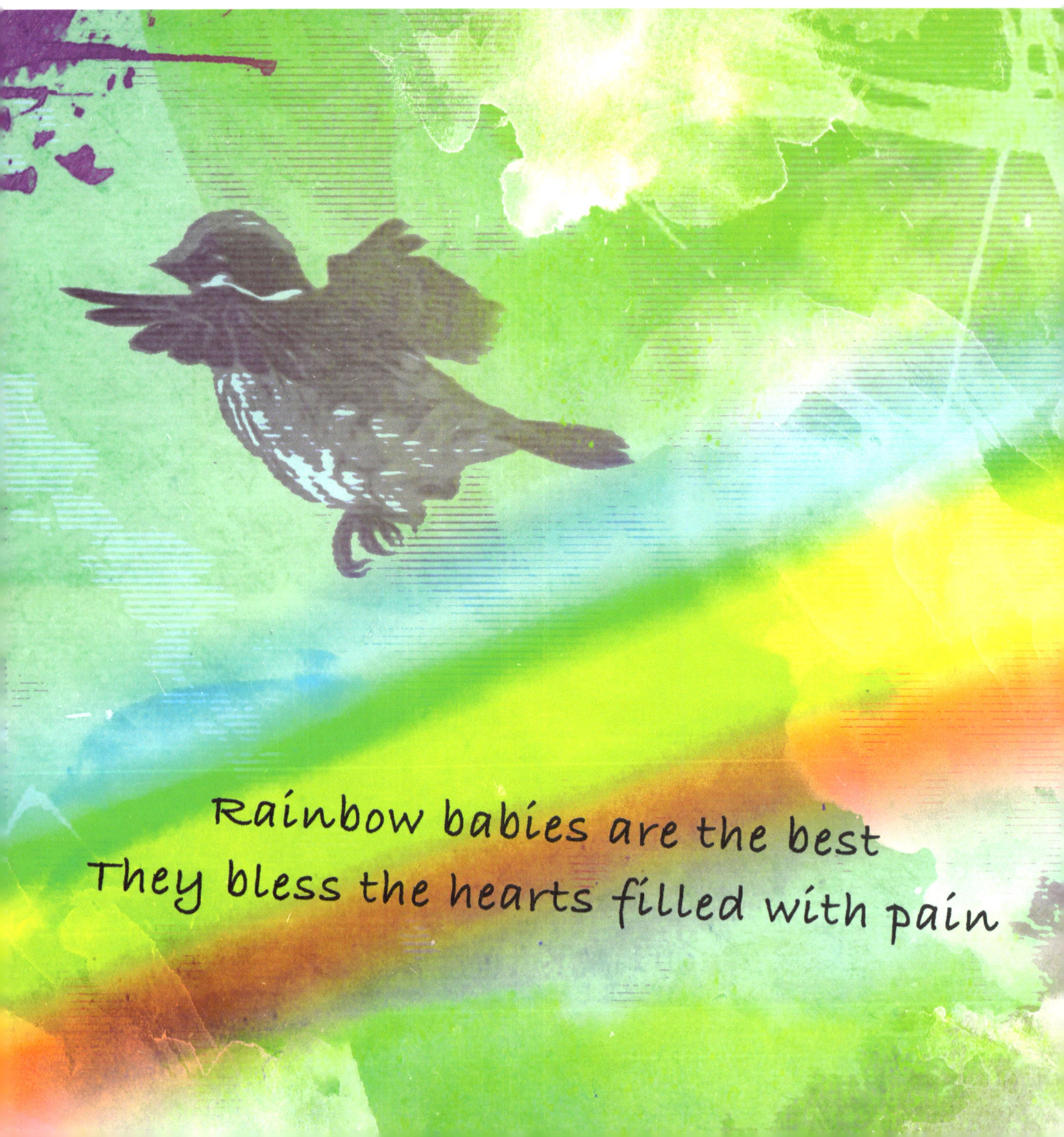

Rainbow babies are the best
They bless the hearts filled with pain

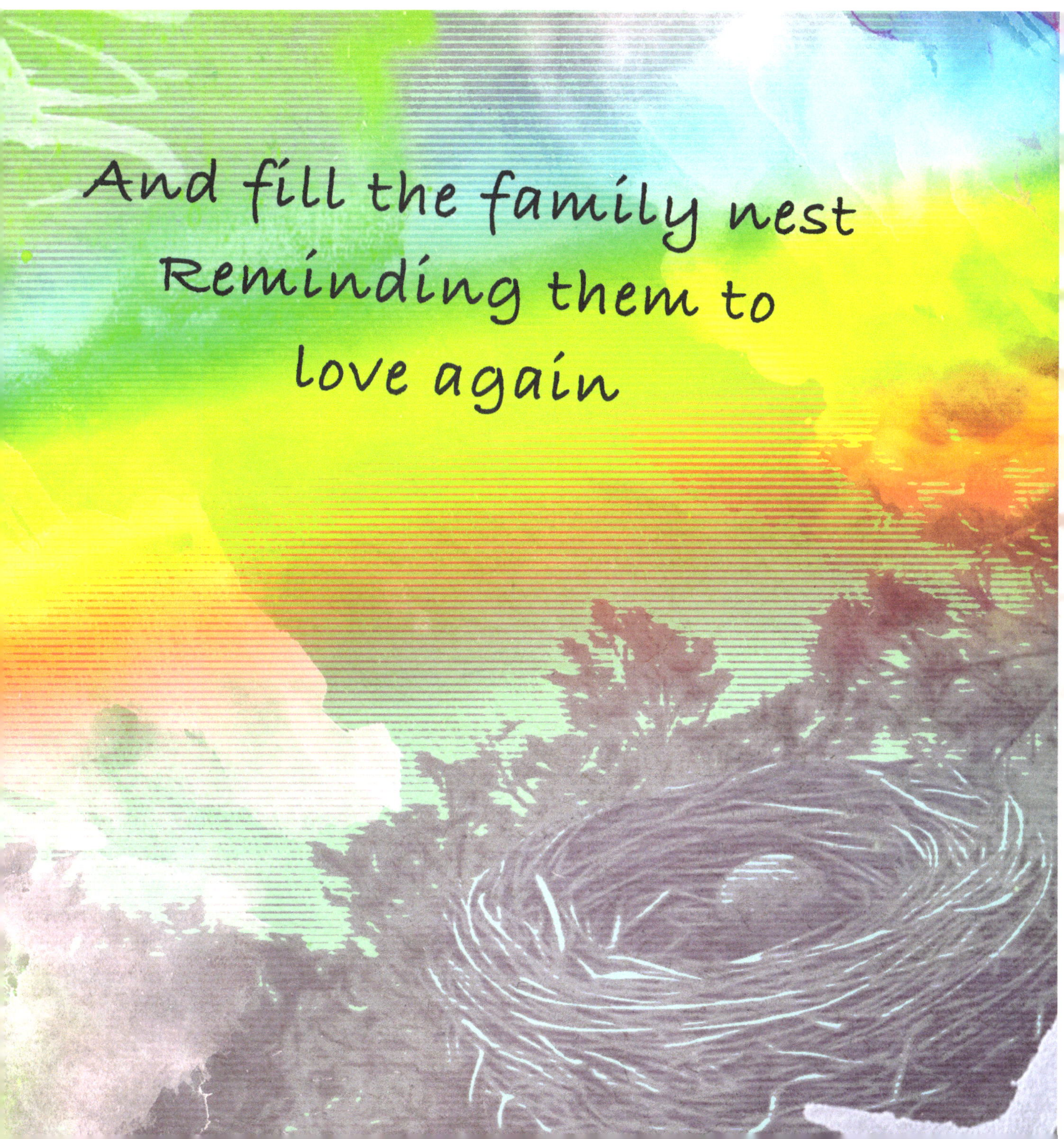
And fill the family nest
Reminding them to
love again